W9-AJL-812

MOVIE MAGIC

ON-SCREEN VEHICLES

BY SARA GREEN

BELLWETHER MEDIA • MINNEAPOLIS, MN

Blastoff! Discovery launches a new mission: reading to learn. Filled with facts and features, each book offers you an exciting new world to explore!

This edition first published in 2020 by Bellwether Media, Inc.

Library of Congress Cataloging-in-Publication Data

Names: Green, Sara, 1964- author.
Title: On-screen vehicles / by Sara Green.
Description: Minneapolis, MN : Bellwether Media, Inc., 2020. | Series: Blastoff! Discovery. Movie Magic | Includes bibliographical references and index.
Identifiers: LCCN 2019000945 (print) | LCCN 2019002718 (ebook) | ISBN 9781618915856 (ebook) | ISBN 9781644870440 (hardcover : alk. paper)
Subjects: LCSH: Motor vehicles in motion pictures–Juvenile literature. | Cinematography–Special effects–Juvenile literature. | Stage props–Juvenile literature.
Classification: LCC PN1995.9.A85 (ebook) | LCC PN1995.9.A85 G74 2020 (print) | DDC 791.43/656–dc23
LC record available at https://lccn.loc.gov/2019000945

Editor: Betsy Rathburn Designer: Brittany McIntosh

Printed in the United States of America, North Mankato, MN.

TABLE OF CONTENTS

VEHICLES IN DISGUISE

A teenage girl makes a surprise discovery in the 2018 film *Bumblebee*. She finds a run-down yellow Volkswagen Beetle in a junkyard. But this is no ordinary car. It is Bumblebee, one of the Transformers!

The Transformers are alien robots that disguise themselves as vehicles. Bumblebee is one of the smaller Transformers. But he is brave and trustworthy. When enemies threaten Bumblebee's life, he must use his wits to survive!

BUMBLEBEE AS A VOLKSWAGON BEETLE

BUMBLEBEE

OPTIMUS PRIME
IN *TRANSFORMERS: REVENGE OF THE FALLEN*

Bumblebee teams up with the rest of the Autobots. They turn into pickup trucks and sports cars. Their leader, Optimus Prime, is a semitruck! They battle the evil Decepticons. These villains can fly through the sky as aircraft!

CGI and real vehicles meet in this film to create all these characters. In *Bumblebee*, the on-screen vehicles are more than just **props**. They take center stage!

WHERE IS BUMBLEBEE?

Bumblebee's disguise is not the same in every Transformers movie. In some movies, he transforms into a yellow Camaro with black stripes!

WHAT ARE ON-SCREEN VEHICLES?

On-screen vehicles are important movie props. Cars, trucks, and airplanes are common in movies. Bicycles, boats, and rockets are often on screen, too!

On-screen vehicles are often placed in the background to set a **scene**. These vehicles help show time and place. For example, the 1978 film *Grease* is set in the 1950s. Back then, cars were longer and wider than today's cars. Street scenes in *Grease* included many of these old cars. They helped tell the audience what **era** the movie was set in!

A FAMOUS MINESWEEPER

One of the most popular films of 1954 was *The Caine Mutiny*. It was set on a U.S. naval ship called the USS *Caine* during World War II.

Vehicles often add excitement to movies. Chase scenes keep the action moving. Explosions add thrills!

Mini Coopers race though the subways of Los Angeles in the 2003 film *The Italian Job*. Enemies on snowmobiles chase James Bond down a mountain in the 1999 film *The World Is Not Enough*. A truck carrying precious cargo speeds through the desert during a chase in *Raiders of The Lost Ark*. Scenes like these keep audiences on the edges of their seats!

CHASING ELEANOR

A 1974 film called *Gone in 60 Seconds* includes a 40-minute car chase. It is one of the longest in film history. The chase focuses on a yellow Ford Mustang called Eleanor.

HISTORY OF ON-SCREEN VEHICLES

The movie **industry** started in the 1890s. Vehicles have played an important role in films ever since! An 1896 film called *Arrival of a Train at La Ciotat* showed a moving train approaching the audience. The film included many camera angles that were groundbreaking at the time.

A 1926 silent film called *The General* also featured a train. Actor Buster Keaton played an **engineer** of a **locomotive** named The General. A famous chase scene ended with the locomotive plunging into a river!

PRICEY PLUNGE

The train chase in *The General* was very expensive to shoot. The scene where the train plunges into the river was the most expensive single shot in the history of silent film!

ON-SCREEN VEHICLE PIONEER

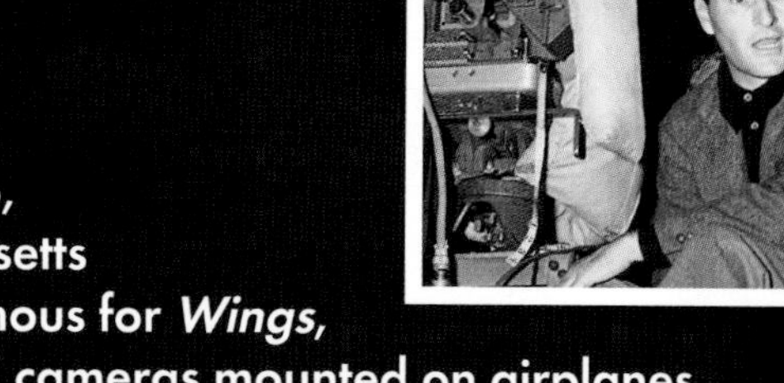

Name: William Wellman
Born: February 29, 1896,
in Brookline, Massachusetts
Known For: Director famous for *Wings*,
a 1927 movie that used cameras mounted on airplanes
to create amazing battle scenes
Awards: Academy Award for Best Story for *A Star Is Born* (1937)

WINGS

THE MAGNIFICENT
AMBERSONS

Cars have also fascinated audiences since the early days of film. The 1927 silent film *The First Auto* is about the shift from horses to cars in the late 1800s. The filmmakers hired a professional race car driver to help develop the racing scenes.

The rise of the automobile industry is also at the center of the 1942 film *The Magnificent Ambersons*. A character named George doubts that people could ever prefer cars over horse-drawn carriages!

COOL COUPE

In the 1950s, the Mercury Coupe was a common family car. Actor James Dean made it cool in the classic 1955 film *Rebel Without a Cause*.

In 1968, two on-screen vehicles were not just part of their movies' stories. They were the stars of their films! A magical race car went on an adventure in the film *Chitty Chitty Bang Bang*. The car, Chitty, could fly in the air and float in the water. When enemies threatened Chitty, it not only saved itself. It also protected the family that loved it!

A Volkswagen racing Beetle named Herbie starred in the 1968 movie *The Love Bug*. This small, clever car overcame great **obstacles** to defeat its competitor!

STORYBOOK CAR

Chitty Chitty Bang Bang **is based on a children's book by Ian Fleming. Fleming also created the character James Bond!**

PET PROJECT

Disney held auditions to find the right car to play Herbie. The casting crew looked at Toyotas, Volvos, and other cars. The Volkswagen Beetle was chosen because it was the only car the crew wanted to pet!

THE LOVE BUG

THE SPY
WHO LOVED ME

Over time, on-screen vehicles continued to advance. Improved technology led to better cars with more features. The James Bond film series is known for its flashy **supercars**. These cars are outfitted with many gadgets. They help James outsmart and outrun his enemies.

In the 1977 film *The Spy Who Loved Me*, James drives a Lotus Esprit S1. Filmmakers used six S1s in the movie. An **engineering** company transformed one of them into a real submarine!

BOMBER BOAT

In the 1979 movie *Moonraker*, James Bond travels by speedboat down the Amazon River. He launches bombs from his boat before he escapes enemies!

Pretend vehicles have made movie history, too. A DeLorean car was also a time machine in the Back to the Future film series. When the car got up to 88 miles (142 kilometers) per hour, it traveled in time. The car vanished in a burst of light!

Each Batman film uses a different Batmobile to fit its story. The 2008 movie *The Dark Knight* featured an armored Batmobile to match the film's **gritty** feel. In 1966, *Batman* featured a unique sports car as the Batmobile. It made the movie look more like a comic book!

GHOST CATCHER

The Ectomobile was featured in the 1984 film *Ghostbusters*. The Ecto-1 was originally a 1959 Cadillac ambulance. It was turned into a ghost-catching machine for the movie!

FAMOUS ON-SCREEN VEHICLE

Name: Batmobile, also called the Tumbler
Movies: *Batman Begins* (2005), *The Dark Knight* (2008), and *The Dark Knight Rises* (2012)
Known For: Vehicle used in three Batman movies and designed to look like a military vehicle, with off-roading tires and carbon fiber panels that allow it to jump roof to roof

CREATIVE EFFECTS

Over time, many films have featured vehicles that were difficult to **shoot**. Filmmakers used creative ways to get them on screen. One method has been the use of models, also called **miniatures**. The *Titanic* appeared as an enormous ship sailing on the sea in the film *Titanic*. A model was used for many scenes.

Miniatures were also used to make the 2018 film *First Man*. Models of the Saturn V rocket and **lunar module** were made using **3D printing**. Designers used NASA **blueprints** to create the models!

TITANIC

MODEL ON THE SET OF *FIRST MAN*

THE FATE
OF THE FURIOUS

Filmmakers also use CGI to create unusual on-screen vehicles. The 2017 film *The Fate of the Furious* features cars racing across an ice field. They must outrun a huge submarine chasing them from beneath the ice. The cars were real, but the submarine was CGI.

The Avengers film series also includes a lot of on-screen vehicles. Some, like Tony Stark's convertible, are real. Others, like Thanos's donut-shaped spaceship, are CGI!

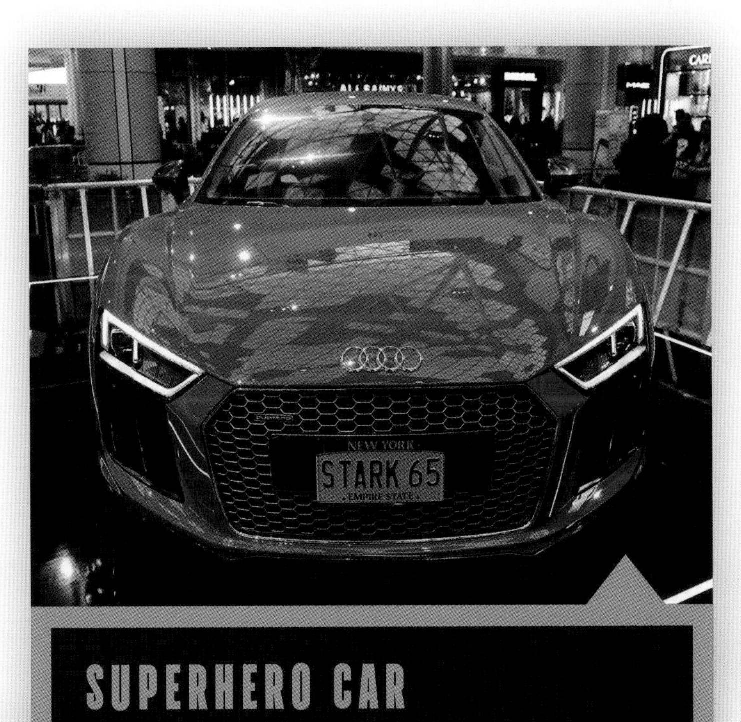

SUPERHERO CAR

Tony Stark drives an Audi R8 Spyder in *Iron Man 2*. The car's top speed is 198 miles (319 kilometers) per hour!

MOVING INTO THE FUTURE

Nobody knows how vehicles will look in the future. But **science fiction** and fantasy films give possible hints.

The Star Wars film series introduced audiences to landspeeders. These vehicles hover over the ground as they move. A Winnebago RV flies through the air in the 1987 science fiction comedy *Spaceballs*. The Starship *Enterprise* from the Star Trek film series transports people to faraway **galaxies**.

STARSHIP *ENTERPRISE*

FAMOUS ON-SCREEN VEHICLE

Name: The Hogwarts Express
Movies: Harry Potter film series (2001-2011)
Known For: A real-life 1937 steam engine that transports students to and from Hogwarts in the Harry Potter film series

CAPTAIN MARVEL

Future on-screen vehicles are sure to offer surprises and thrills. Some will be real, like many of the airplanes in *Captain Marvel*. Filmmakers will continue using CGI to create imaginary vehicles, too!

Future on-screen vehicles may be made by printers instead of factories. A 3D-printed supercar called the Blade was first printed in 2015. It goes from 0 to 60 miles (97 kilometers) per hour in 2.2 seconds! Real or make-believe, on-screen vehicles promise to jump-start the action!

THE BLADE

GLOSSARY

3D printing—the process of making an object in which models are scanned and printed using many thin layers of materials stacked on top of one another

blueprints—illustrations of buildings, vehicles, and other objects that describe how they should be built

CGI—artwork created by computers; CGI stands for computer-generated imagery.

engineer—a person who is in charge of a train

engineering—the use of science and math to design and create buildings, cars, and other objects

era—a period of time known for particular developments

galaxies—systems of millions of stars

gritty—dark or rough

industry—a group of businesses that provide a certain product

locomotive—a powered rail vehicle that pulls trains

lunar module—a small craft used for traveling between the moon's surface and an orbiting spacecraft

miniatures—small models

obstacles—things that block the way

props—short for properties; props are the objects used by actors or set decorators in movies.

scene—the action in a single place and time in a film or play

science fiction—made up stories based on future science; science fiction often features space and life on other planets.

shoot—the act of filming a movie

supercars—luxury, high-performance sports cars

TO LEARN MORE

AT THE LIBRARY

Green, Sara. *Stunts*. Minneapolis, Minn.: Bellwether Media, 2019.

Oachs, Emily Rose. *Aston Martin DB9*. Minneapolis, Minn.: Bellwether Media, 2017.

Omoth, Tyler. *Incredible Car Stunts*. North Mankato, Minn.: Capstone Press, 2016.

ON THE WEB

FACTSURFER

Factsurfer.com gives you a safe, fun way to find more information.

1. Go to www.factsurfer.com.
2. Enter "on-screen vehicles" into the search box and click 🔍.
3. Select your book cover to see a list of related web sites.

INDEX

The images in this book are reproduced through the courtesy of: Gareth Davies/ Getty, front cover, p. 21; Paramount Pictures/ Everett Collection, pp. 4, 5; Jaimie Trueblood/ Paramount/ Everett Collection, p. 6; Sarunyu L, p. 7; Everett Collection, pp. 8, 11, 13 (bottom), 14, 18; TCD/ Prod.DB/ Alamy, pp. 9, 22, 23, 24; Paramount/ Everett Collection, pp. 10, 26; Photo 12/ Alamy, pp. 12, 16; Glasshouse Images/ Alamy, p. 13 (top); Mary Evans/ Ronald Grant/ Everett Collection, p. 15; Buena Vista Pictures/ Photofest Digital, p. 17; United Artists/ Everett Collection, p. 19; AF archive/ Alamy, p. 20; PA Images/ Alamy, p. 25; Ian Rutherford/ Alamy, p. 27; Chuck Zlotnick/ Walt Disney Studios Motion Pictures/ Marvel/ Everett Collection, p. 28; Divergent Technologies, p. 29.